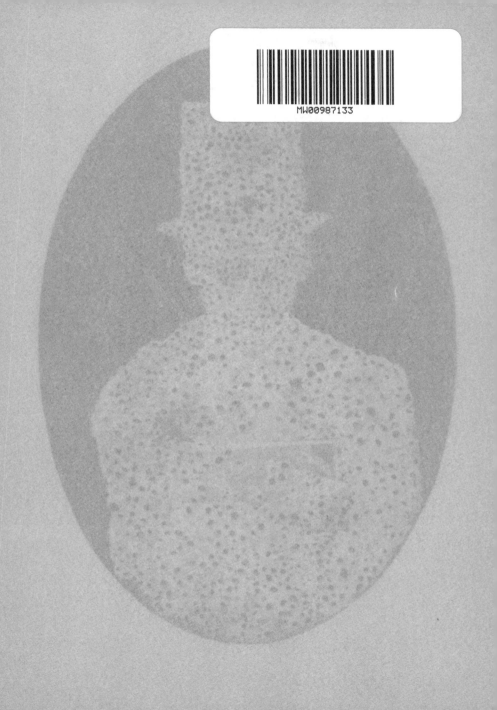

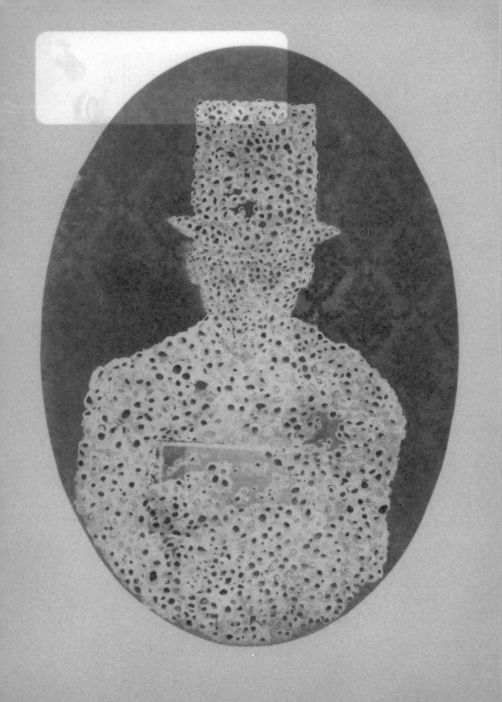

The Youngest Butcher in Illinois

Also from YesYes Books

Please Don't Leave Me Scarlett Johansson
by Thomas Patrick Levy

Heavy Petting by Gregory Sherl

Panic Attack, USA by Nate Slawson

I Don't Mind If You're Feeling Alone
by Thomas Patrick Levy

Pepper Girl by Jonterri Gadson

If I Should Say I Have Hope by Lynn Melnick

Poetry Shots
a digital chapbook series

Nocturne Trio
with poetry by Metta Sama and art by Mihret Dawit

Toward What Is Awful
with poetry by Dana Guthrie Martin and art by Ghangbin Kim

How to Survive a Hotel Fire
with poetry by Angela Veronica Wong and art by Megan Laurel

The Blue Teratorn
with poetry by Dorothea Lasky and art by Kaori Mitsushima

My Hologram Chamber Is Surrounded by Miles of Snow
with poetry by Ben Mirov and images by Eric Amling

The Youngest Butcher in Illinois

by Robert Ostrom

YesYes Books ❧❧ Blacksburg, VA

The Youngest Butcher in Illinois by Robert Ostrom

Printed in the United States of America

Cover Art: "Self-Portrait with Barnacles" by Dan Estabrook

Cover and Interior Design: K.M.A. Sullivan

Lead Editor: Justin Boening

First Edition
978-1-936919-09-3

Published by YesYes Books
814 Hutcheson Drive
Blacksburg, VA 24060
YesYesBooks.com

for my family

CONTENTS

BONE MAP

Here is the sweetgum in dirt. Here are the bones

rearticulated. In mourning of great event,

in leaf mulch, a hoop earring with no back.

Hope is your old love long past

a bridge with orange tassels. Tremble

and birds peal from a culvert. Here, at the base

of a ridge, a necklace in a seasonal creek.

Baling twine and emery cloth. What waits

in pines, what, with small sounds, grates teeth

is unremarkable. And you can't breathe.

From Time to Time by the Skin of Your Face

Things past tumble back, thoughts gather
thoughts: dreadnaught, thickset, a roman
candle. It is a bedroom that wants
a southern addition; it swelters and finds
license. Idle hands, young shoulder, sweat lines
from a neck to a back, a father stitching
the wound in his arm before it can finish
what it was saying about the godseat. Or was it
the goblet? Numinous iota, I dare you. Race
to the pilings and back. Like ants bearing mint
across a white counter, it is too much
of a good thing. Nostalgia, the distance a sigh
travels before reaching its source. A torment
disguised as reverie. It is written on the side
of my skull. Did I have a twin? I had notions
that part of me grew toward the earth.

To His Nephew

In my bureau is a matchbox. I am not going to make this easy for you. In the box there are two cloves, a snip of lavender, and a piece of ribbon. Inside the ribbon, a girl walks tiptoe with outstretched arms past the living room. She is my grandmother. In her pocket, a cinnamon quill and kitchen shears; in the bend of her arm, kith and kin: her grandfather carefully opens a butterfly case in which the inner ears of mammals are pinned. From the skein of bones like shell he hears something like metal and bird in a hallway. I am telling you because you want to be told. It's the clinking (do you hear) of a pocket case, minor operating instruments in an old man's hand. He runs toward his wife who braces herself on the spiral baluster. Around her neck they say she wore a bite of arsenic, but I know inside the pendant her mother sleeps beside my eldest sister. Tonight, you will sleep in your room because you are tired and because you do not believe me.

Put Right One Might Say It Was Your Own Fault

Plucked out of marl and mud, patched up and paraded; parading, as seabirds on dry land, palpable indecision. Like gnats, thoughts came forward often, to nag often or pretend to be holy. Untied elephants. Then a shrieking like a mandrake, asking, who unto me do I deem my boss? Who with golden surmise? To make disorder but to show stability, the goal was always to diminish and hit right, then retreat, advance, break again what they support. So in the branches in your skin, they went looking for you. In place of your eyes they found foxholes and hoary days. Or was it prowling anticipation that tied me up in this tree?

Distress in This Cautionary Tale Is Dirt on the Lips

I am two nurseries. Beside a box of ornaments the smallest organs reside, useful, barely, to the cataloguing flesh, an able choir. But what chews at my stomach? Another rain ruins another family musical. Who unbuttons? Birds point to my body and birds point to trees so woodlands flourish in these walls. The branches point to a prisoner: a girl beside the mouth of a lake looks downstream and waves. She has been dreaming of cities, dresses, the early moustache of a young man.

Someday she will test the depth. I walk to that selfsame edge.

The lake is a heavy coat. Pines sing. On her ribs she can feel the pulse of a pocketwatch in my grandfather's vest (chained not only to each other) because our ilk-dream rummages in the tops of trees, high above these walls, but just below my lung resigns itself to paper cranes. Cement cranes. Falls to pieces. Rests and rests once. Under the grape arbor, I would like to think.

It Is Not What I Have but I Bring It

On our backs in pine
needles with dirty feet and
whale pleasures I swear
endlessly inside; with
affection with one of
God's hairs; mandate
brazen. To choose the
color of the bikeshed.
Who stands outside
hears rummaging within.
Impermanence pedals
around a child. How much
colder can it get and still
sway and purse and touch.

The Pause That It Makes

This is the sound of a foreman driving the last of his nails into comfort, a voice to another, or a horse falling down a flight of stairs. In my thumb, a splinter from the bed frame, the bed frame's tree. In my other hand, a frozen finch; a horse or this is the sound of a man ripping all the doors from a house (it's just his way of saying he misses you). How he loves to watch us swim in those round-cornered photographs. He can't stop thinking about you. Standing on the banks of the shore, mayflies in the cattails, I wake to the sound of your body molting; a horse or you drown in one vacation after another, colorless, falling to the bottom, your hair uncoils your head as your eyes open then turn upward to see at length a rising blonde cloud and beyond, familiar faces ascending.

A Dedication to the Rich Is in the Ark

He knew they'd dig up his masks
and throw out his counsel:
a herringbone coat, cranes
in a turnip field: men disguised
as weeping, white birds. His childhood
home, where dust had grown to fur,
would take but five pregnant minutes
to burn to dirt. Written on the back
of a photo in which he poses
below a twisted phoenix, fuck charters
and fuck fireworks. He never wanted
to be a fold-up theater; he wanted
to eat sturgeon from the Black
Sea. He worked a while stacking chairs
in a church auditorium. A pile of what
skeletons, he thought. He wore an amethyst
bracelet. A chemical would maintain
him for a time. Until death, like a whim.

A Third Possibility

Homesick, homesick, worldsmart.
Software and a cantaloupe. All these
joys have alibis. Are handled.

A Boy Cupping a Cricket Turns to Us and Says

A sled with too many reins
to go anywhere, my father who is not

my father sews my hands together. Around

a table where the people resemble, dazzled
like horses staring at each other. We ate

mixed berries with sugar. The bower bloomed

under which it was always cold in my hair.
There was an Easter morning. Every question

was the same question. Until the house

began to speak. Then, the skin of your face
in a box of old faces. Where you made

mouths in the grass, you made mirrors

of me. Suffering impersonating suffering,
the evening routine of little brown bats.

I Hereby Declare You Island of Dogs

I hereby attest I am unable to know what will come next or even what has come next in the past, except to say, I might have thought in a moment of weakness that my English was of a free impulse, I mean my nature, and tender and would therefore pilot me to sustainability and Christendom.

To say that I am exclusively interested in your miseries is true. My mouth, my steer, I have heard that in March all bear cubs are stillborn but their mothers lick them to life. I have learned the way a conversation can stumble in and out of prayer. How, in abandoned bedrooms, there is the sensation that things must still go in order, things next to things, each with its own essence.

Because I am in a region from which, some nights, I can hear the barking of waves, what floats in the blood like a splinter, I am a village without a church. And the dogs lick me, they eye me. I have called on you today because there are questions that beg answering. When I return I will look you up and tell you to meet me at such and such a place; then, upon seeing me, you will employ expressions of concern and in your gentler voice you will say, my dear, you have grown so much faster than your cage.

TO SHOW THE LIVING

Provide a picture of your habitat.

An amble in pennyroyal,
Catchweed, cusp of sleep. Kitchen
Or highway. Floodlit
And combustible agriculture.
Mornings in thrall, evenings
Handled by other eyes. A playroom
Floor, quiet house. The poverty
Of our credo, ax handle, civil. One
Can hear scratching of locusts in their eggs
At the edge of the lake. The apostate is
Memorysick, rouge on his pillow.
At the edge of slumber one can sense
The edge of a lake. We are not safe here.

Define properties (invisible).

There   are your offhands
and ill-rehearsed   when the timbre

of faces   scatter

Night withdraws its kettledrums
of lips and skin   when loss

finds you   after pitch, the resin

Tell about going on a journey and what you would carry with you.

Quilts, thirty. Dresses.

To take the skin off, to take my hair
all off, three and one ready blade.

Was given away.   And went.
What I take with me: this house, its

swarm; body my horse.   Past north

work over tall grass. To the noise of cut
rue. This is where you find me.

Describe the noises that it makes.

knee-deep in snow and dead
                    yarrow but what makes you
            cold (these needs inherit needs)
            a boil of birds the sound of
    larvae in the trees in lodgepole pines
            past the switchyard the crash
                    of coupling trains

Tell me the kinds of work a person does.

Relinquish. Ransom. Repairwork.

Repair, skins. Relinquish, restless. Ransom, some
prayer. Repair, hair. Relinquish, pawn. Relinquish, her
dresses. Ransom, temper. Repair, a third. Ransom,
for house. Relinquish, for mother. Ransom, the rest.
Relinquish, your arms. Ransom, your legs. Repair,
chorus of hair. Relinquish, drudgery. Ransom, pocket
of earth. Ransom, risk and weather. Repair, flesh in the
grass. Repair, where her troubles gather. Relinquish.

Tell me what happens to things you own.

Define properties (visible).

What is the right way for a family to live?

Near a nest of red
Bluebirds I left
The body of a man
Wrapt carelessly
In birchbark.

Describe the noises that it makes.

Pennies   falling
from a hand   -ful of pennies.

Provide a picture of your habitat.

We traveled to a coast I had never been to before, nor since. I had never seen the sea and when we arrived we arrived in dark so that, as my father and I walked toward the beach (I was afraid we would drown), it seemed as if the tide was at our feet and, during that night, the sound of water, angry, reached into my sleep. In the morning I could see: a hill leading to moorland which farther off became sand but the ocean as always was distantly inaudible.

How do you teach a girl the things she should know?

In backyard first

        stones then diagrams
of stones   Fist-bones

their providence

Half-grown wing
knives the ground

Broken jaw record
      of contingency

      The worst returns
to tinsel
      the comic hinge
      of fracture

In the dawn-lit cornfield

      a cellar door opens

In My Father's Kingdom

This Is the Record of John

The first time I thought
about hitting her
I thought of those nuns

who, with their absurd
hands, float
strategically to hymn

machines. On an ornamental
hilltop in West Virginia
I felt someone build a nest

in my mouth. I tore my shirt
at a stranger's funeral
(blessed is the one true judge).

How sunlight I thought
can yellow the hemline
of a dress. How gravel

can settle a body. And by
gravel I mean, here,
I give you all my clouds.

Comb back your hair.

Please Lord, Do Not Hunt Me

Some people said that the horses ran into bonfires and wolf
spiders ate their mothers. Caged crows were known to mimic the
voices of humans; stray cats, in search of food, died crossing the
harbor. For a while it seemed it was all for nothing. For hope, we
blended myths with our known truths. We knew the hair of the
dead continued to grow, but did buried babies learn to talk? We
grew confused. Am I a horse or a crow? My grandfather was a
grave so I am a grave. Livestock waited for delivery in pens at the
station. You will not be back, they said. Christ, look at the stars, the
houses, the child at the stove! Some people ran into bonfires, and
some people buried their mothers while others tried to speak but
they kept saying the same thing: over and over.

Fetish

Where the other half
Of my humor

Is familiar, darlings rage
Days numbered and dark-

Skinned, an orange
I pare in the morning

To find another of her hairs
Even this is providential

Forgive me my salt
My crowded temper

My hand enacted here
Is vainglory and wishful

Unpaired earrings
Sit in a drawer beside my bed

The Pause That It Makes

Because crows in the bracken

In the after-light

Because deluge, wasp-loud eave

Because restless, despite camphor, sepia scene

For bewildering, scythe and self and glean

Tree-of-heaven in brume

By this, to nest in fog, all dew

Fore and aft the hive, their paper wings

Because cold, the grass, green bedlam

I mean, dwells inside the body, undoings

Despite outside; flax and the sleepless birds

Beehive (Thimble Forest)

I gave her a blonde-haired doll. She said, be careful, someday your doll will kill your dog. I give you, Sofia, my good portions. In the near new future, there will be no more dolor, all your valleys will blush and disappear the way flintlocks lit the faces of soldiers. One night, under Sofia, a spider nested in my beard and, as it worked, I heard it mumble, make her a parakeet as small as the cup of your palm, husk her of possibility until she stirs like a cave. Sofia, the one lit room in a dark house. Sofia, the jockey lost his way. Let us speak frankly, she'd say, until only the verbs remain. In your woods. Sofia, bar the door.

The Arms Are the Unblest Among Tools

You won't forget the grass, a cloud of insects
as loud as if a thought had risen from the roots

of your teeth: a woman as old as her son
is as cutlery to plow. After all you forget touch, hair

and the light of it, the weight of a waking body. Near
a nest of red bluebirds, I left the body of a man wrapt

carelessly in birch bark. What you wanted to say
was his skin. Which means ruth and harvesting.

Confessions of a Forest Fire

Once again someone has disquieted the country dogs.

I woke this morning, precocious, full of edges.

I woke and found a deer inside my bedroom.

A dirt road lined with pulsating horses.

(A small house is the metaphor for anything.)

And the woods? A small house of clamoring hours.

Woman, small house feeding its will,

Let's go back to my room.

I am heady with chestnut leaves and I am tired of talking.

You have given birth to so many ghosts.

When I leave, imagine a house empty

But for one broken chair, an injured swan.

When I am gone, you will be unrecognizable.

Which Their Own Conduct Has, in the Past, Exposed

And now his to her. Inside the halls of the woman one can witness nights as the dying must. And he will. Anyone would have guessed the small fires in his hand were to keep sight not of her face but his way there. Anyone could see that though the house was stately, they lived wholly in one room. That he would cut her out of dull scenery and risk a quandary of ice is true but he is with the occasion of fall—when he lay down with her she bore him a garden: wooden shells, green eyes that hung like watchbells on eves. He knows her ways and she knows a hand upon a hand before a face is a room where he can become his animal. He will hide his bones on cedar rafters; they have long been his and must remain his. Much affected, but she will forgive, though alone, and he will bestow his energy on some other endeavor. I should make myself my own house, he says. He'd sooner stand in less than this uneasy manor.

Is Another Appear

In a glass room in the tree ferns. Sleeping,
a frond stretches its legs. Lady and salvaged
furniture. I want to take so much. Air
fern is an animal dyed green. Amanita,
freckled skin hidden in the mossery, veiled
truffles on a communion tray. The lake
is in the sky and belowground, some bodies
once loved on their featherbeds. Rheumy-eyed,
dolorous, typical. In caverns of misplaced sentiment
they linger but she is already big as a starling
in the fallible night, in a head made of windows.

Three Act Structure

A Calvinist is
hiding in my
attic. I wouldn't
want anyone
to come back.

Animus

Whatever was said was said

with so much ease

and nobody went looking
                    All birds flew

and furthermore
You were there

And there are so many cities in a bird

Funerary Stele with Farewell Scene

At last I let go of the heavy balloon and watched as it floated simply away. There are rivers to some cities, he told me. Hands in my sleeves, I was smaller than I thought: the balloon passed over bridges and minarets but I could've been anywhere: the snow on the barges and on the Bosporus was just the snow in my hair and the call to prayer, the last pariah dogs gathering; we're upstairs, they said, and even if we don't comfort you, join us, and risk us as friends. I was smaller than my thoughts: taking his hand, I followed to a thin island where dogs lined the coast. Dressed in my father's fatigues, I felt so useful! In his tongue, my voice was an empty house, I spoke but no one replied except for the dogs whose laughter dissipated in the distance. A breeze upturned a little fog: a broken boat, an empty coat. When I woke, I washed the dishes, placed the colored bowls in the sun, and watered the pansies. Once again I rearranged my apartment: the photo of the barge, the large one-eyed balloon. Nothing could be the same, I thought. In a dialect not my own.

The Youngest Butcher in Illinois

Heretofore he watches the last
of the hour ooze into thirsty
sleep. Wait, head. Stayawhile. Doll
blood on his hands. Under streets
the city can almost hear a passing over,
children in the leaves. And the leaves
they leave through his mouth. Inside
the body, foreign bodies: the season
steals about his brain, his weigh
station. The house-staff are panic-
stricken. His histrionics taste like
apples. Hello trial. Hello betrothed.
Attaboy.

TO SHOW THE LIVING

What is done after a person dies?

One flies and several erupt from a tree.
One flies alone, like a girl, chased
And disappears into a field
Of bluestem. Would you say angelic?
Our sleeping heads murmur with many
Arms reaching. A cousin is drowning
In revels under the bridge. Gregarious,
Locusts feeding on the orchard. Migration
Dreams agitate these knuckles, our bony
Wings. Another city is a face stitched
To an eye. Kitchen or highway? In rain
Our wings smell more dog than divine.

Provide a picture of your home.

Lead paint peels in the bedroom (crows in a field of poppies). Tree rings. Years of linoleum. Dishes in the sink. Mother still hangs on the wall. A cradle and tattered linens. Scissors in molasses. Sleep then. Bats. Owls. Large cat. Sister twists her hair around her finger. Gently singing in the driveway. Waiting patiently. Black shutters. Maple roots are organ pipes at a wedding. Legs tucked into a nightshirt. Briars. Nests in the eaves. Look at the mice. How they look away. Take no heed. Weevils in the flour jar. Nightjars in the aspen. Stuffing themselves with the sound of moths. Know by the cry in the stand past the field. Know the field. Crow field. Violet is field.

Tell what happens to widows.

Before we were whales and far in green, she was taller here, walking the flat with me at low tide. Letting go my hand, she'd stoop, drive hers into the sand and, pulling out a razor, rinse it and say, "dear, here." Sandy, I'd suck them out of those long shells she held to my lips. Her hair was bay leaves and kale, much yearned for. Skin, silver then gone not to harvest bogs or rake quahogs in deep, but such a distance that her children's landscape (black pudding, milksweet coffee), was not her landscape. Winters this long she'd pickle everything until spring when, in thimbleweed, so inland she lost sight then salt and will not be back.

Provide a picture of your home.

Because field is hue of body.

Define its properties (visible).

It is snowing here.

It is snowing everywhere.

Tell how you would give a gift to a man.

Fill your pockets with dirt and the nights

you visit me, unknowingly,

may your plans be downright

unseen, your palms face-down,

may you be more favored; stranger,

bring me water. For forgiveness.

Describe the noises that it makes.

With our trucks and dogs, with cured meat and care, in a field of aster we drink Budweiser. Where the plow cuts back toward the street, past a dead oak we call Endeavor, a fire, singing, and laughter.

Tell what cannot be told.

Believe me you will miss

The noises   your window   the traffic   and errands
Commonplace   keepsakes   your hands   in time

You will fail to remember the color of Mother's eyes

Tell about going on a journey and what you would carry with you.

Provide a picture of your habitat.

My sister and I pick raspberries.

62

What is done after a person dies?

Where you fingered the worn decades of your rosary, a bushel of weeds has been overturned. The dill you'd gather in your robe rose to the window. In the garden, in the soil, coiled around a root, one of your hairs. Livid, I ate the onions that were growing out of proportion. Last week I saw a stranger help a blind man to a rotating door. The way he must go alone. I took to heart. For him I've catalogued each hand in a day and the different ways color comes to a face. I have found abundance in enumeration. Glory be tangled in the thickest part of the rose, a bed spring then your face seemed so near the window. World without end, was it worth it? Even now your heath spreads and the oak dismantles. Nor was there ever any window.

What sort of things belong to a family?

I have been weighing my eminent
debts against the governance of small

talk. Georgina cuts the tulips under
her catalpa or my grandfather

was a tulip in the shadow of more rigid
arms. The sad work of parents, or was it just

the residue of a black walnut?

Provide a picture of your habitat.

The small veins behind a boy's ear.

Which is to say?

A window and, outside it, two strays.

And outside them?

Seven horses eating green from their hooves.

Which is to say?

You moved through my body without touching my body.

ABOUT THE AUTHOR

Robert Ostrom is from Jamestown, New York. He is the author of two chapbooks, *To Show the Living* (The New York Center for Book Arts) and *Nether and Qualms* (Projective Industries). His poems have appeared in *Columbia: A Journal of Literature and Art, Gulf Coast,* and *Cut Bank,* among other journals. He lives in Queens and teaches at the City University of New York and Columbia University.

ACKNOWLEDGMENTS

I would like to thank the editors of the following for publishing some of the work that appears in this book: *42opus, Glitterpony, Drunken Boat, CutBank, Gulf Coast, Columbia: A Journal of Literature and Art, Vinyl, Phantom Limb, Verse Daily, InDigest: Poem of the Day Podcast, The Helen Burns Poetry Anthology: New Voices from the Academy of American Poets*, and *Flying Guillotine's Apocalypse Anthology*. Portions were published in the chapbook, *Nether and Qualms*, from Projective Industries. I am grateful to the New York Center for Book Arts and especially to Sharon Dolin and Tomaž Šalamun for choosing *To Show the Living* for their 2008 chapbook prize.

I am indebted to all my teachers, many of whom are also my friends, family, and students. There are far too many to mention here, so I will gratefully acknowledge those who have directly influenced the making of this book.

For their correspondence, feedback and enthusiasm, I thank Pranav Behari, Thomas Hummel, Carey McHugh, Melissa Ostrom, Addie Palin, and Andrew Seguin. My grandfather, William Hershberger, provided flora, animal, and other instruction. The CATWALK Residency gave me time for reflection. I thank K.M.A. Sullivan for her vigilant handling of this book. Further thanks to Timothy Donnelly for his generosity and guidance. For his editorial suggestions and belief in this work, I will always be grateful to Justin Boening.

Finally, I offer my deepest gratitude to Lucie Brock-Broido, shepherdess and alibi.

NOTES

Bone Map

"Distress in This Cautionary Tale Is Dirt on the Lips" uses imagery inspired by the photographs of Charles Van Schaick.

The title "It Is Not What I Have but I Bring It" is from *Louise Bourgeois: Drawings and Observations*.

The description of the horse in "The Pause That It Makes" reflects a scene in Andrei Tarkovsky's 1966 film, *Andrei Rublev*.

"A Third Possibility" borrows a line from Max Ernst's *A Little Girl Dreams of Taking the Veil*.

"I Hereby Declare You Island of Dogs" refers to the island of Oxia and draws from the late 14th century *Livre de chasse* (*Book of Hunting*) by Gaston Phoebus.

To Show the Living

The elicitations in these sections were inspired by and, at times, appropriated from Nancy Hickerson's *Vocabulary List and Queries for Eliciting* found in Dorthea Kaschube's 1950's anthropological monograph, *Crow Texts*, in which Kaschube interviews Henrietta Pretty on Top, a young member of the Crow Nation. The sections also owe a debt to the morphological transcriptions and phonetic translations of Pretty on Top's responses. These sections are dedicated in memory of my grandmother, Georgina Ostrom.

NOTES (cont.)

In My Father's Kingdom

The title "Please Lord, Do Not Hunt Me" refers to Job 10:16.

"Beehive (Thimble Forest)" is the title of a Joseph Cornell box. Some of the language is from Vladimir Nabokov's "A Busy Man" from *Details of a Sunset*.

The title "The Arms Are the Unblest Among Tools" is from Susuki's translation of the *Tao Te Ching* by Lao Tzu.

The title "Which Their Own Conduct Has, in the Past, Exposed" and some of the lines in this poem are from *David Copperfield* by Charles Dickens.

"Is Another Appear" is for Diana Gruberg.

"Funerary Stele with Farewell Scene" is the title of a Greek sculpture (5 BC) housed in the Istanbul Archaeological Museum. This poem also alludes to the island of Oxia. A couple of lines were adapted from John Berryman's "Despair" in *Love and Fame*.

The title poem, "The Youngest Butcher in Illinois," is for Pranav Behari.